WILDFLOWER HELL

AMALGAMATED POEMS

TANYA RAKH

Worms and dogs and blinding highways. The day the words had no more time. Just a minute, cemeteries. All the open love a living sore.

—from "seashells"

*where the rivers bleed
in every color
and no one can find us*

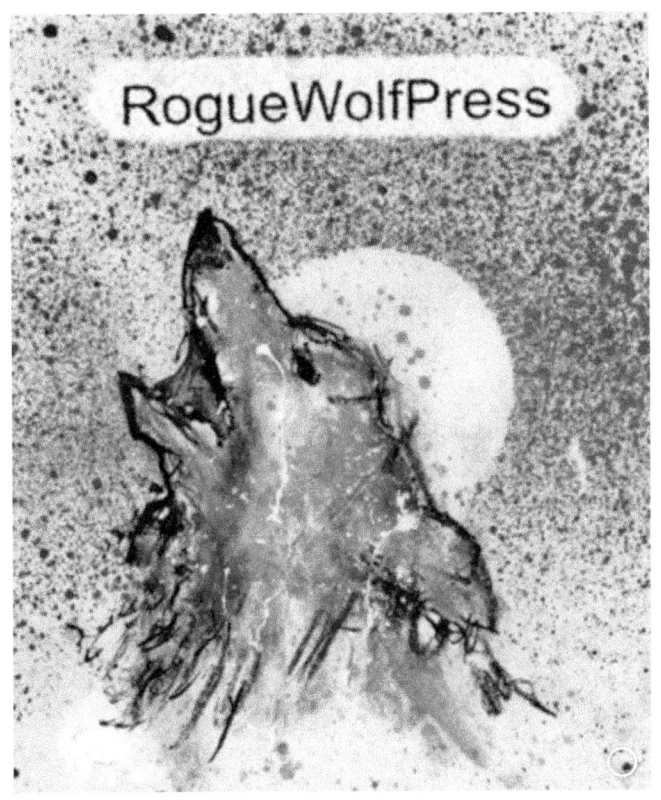

Published by Rogue Wolf Press ©®
Tanya Rakh © 2021
Cover Art by Wolf Kevin Martin ©

All Rights Reserved. No part of this book may be reproduced or transmitted in any form or by any means without written permission from the author.

ACKNOWLEDGEMENTS

"always in love," "seashells," and "that summer" published in *Literary Orphans*

"angel hell," "laps," "oceans," "spool," and "the star side (it flew back)" published in *Danse Macabre*

"etchings on the golem of fallen stars" and "breathe" published in *DM du Jour*

"easier" published in *The Rye Whiskey Review*

"need" published in *The Smoking Typewriter*

"subtext" and "lean back" published in *1870*

WILDFLOWER HELL

**I. winter
black-lacquered roses**

woman as bedsore, trampled by violets
always in love
seashells
arachnid
subtext
need
wildflowers
it flew away
seasons will change

**II. spring
baby's breath, broken concrete**

ripe
lily
Persephone
leaf
faescapes
oceans
etchings on the golem of fallen stars
quiet
midnight
we can be stars now

III. summer
violets in blind sun

that summer
voices
lean back
angel hell
easier
the open road
laps
hell
breathe

IV. fall
hibiscus, orange-red

your blood
spool
hello
you die alone
the star side (it flew back)
pinhead
flower moon
flightless
worlds
always

For you

all stories are true
all magic is real

**I. winter
black-lacquered roses**

woman as bedsore, trampled by violets

now you see her
now you taste
everything as ash

she says mauve
she says thunder
you stay a kettle on
an electric memory

my heart is not rotten
I know because it looks
just like yours

always in love

always my love, an invasive species
I am always in love
always in love, a crimson candle
the skinned girl skinned knees,
looking down

burgundy stain on satin landscape
silver minutes stretching by
vines crawl up, open the cruel door
nature takes back her memories
swallows the blood again

you come to me a single flicker
light within my darkened bruises
kaleidoscope, you tell me
primary colors flash your eyes and I am
half-eaten
clinging to ether,
against dark branches

in the fires, love, we always find this
ten million locks of hair,
all our war-torn cemeteries
water through our mired scar tissue
yes this, the melting point
the promise,
our bruises spreading into stars

always in love, the final arrow,
a black lung breathing out the time

seashells

And when the words have no more time, time hardens as a crystal. Numb my eyes I twist live sidewalks past ceramic dawn. Past the cemeteries of all our dead lovers; they just brood and smoke cigars now, cast dirty snow by dumpster blaze.

Warm your hands and sit with me, my head is full of stars and night went cold already. Meet me over a single candle, please ignore the drip in my sad rooftops, all my tin silverware clatters with passing trains. Look at me and we can swallow. These muscles can unravel here.

Maybe through the fear. Maybe through red curtains. Maybe past eleven dogs down this gray alley, littered clean with plastic legs. Don't tell me about fear now, I know one side at least—lifelong and throbbing, hollow seashells of euphoria.

Don't tell me about seashells, don't tell me about grief. Don't tell me about parchment lining old mouths in my home country. Don't tell me about the dancing girls again, I listened to the songs but now I'm hungry. Always hungry. Worms and dogs.

Worms and dogs and blinding highways. The day the words had no more time. Just a minute, cemeteries. All the open love a living sore.

Lie with me a cavern glow. An arm, at least, a hole to swim through. Paint with me a doorway, a gash in monotone night. I always fall asleep here. Somewhere here. A doorway and a wild rose. Some wilted signatures. One shadow. Our cryogenic, humming sky.

arachnid

my heart is a thousand loyal spiders
a million eyes
I am a love that spits and drowns

held afloat by eyelashes
the promises of a thousand spider webs
glistening syllables
spinning me home

we are the monsters we hide from
under covers
under stars

subtext

Anyway . . . (any
way. all ways. show
me how to do it)

Always (bone and fire
and sky and—)

Fuck. (under starlit
days dried into
hope and vapor)

Fuck it. (all falls down
as ashes. better
luck next—)

Tomorrow (all dust and
cyclone steady as
it disappears)

lol (two-headed jesters
flicker weary tongues)

So . . . (show me how
to do it. slowly
please
this time.)

Okay. (fuck you. any
way)

need

I need to taste
your every scar and follicle.
Each aria cluster,
these ripe constellations.

I need to belong to you.
Our roots woven under
forest and lavender.

Come and dream inside me.
Hold me alive where we belong.

wildflowers

cover me in wildflowers
bring me home inside
your sorrow,
all your years of grief
and strain

hold me close and let me
pull your heart inside

I want to bathe in
all your stories
all your heavens,
each flower hell

it flew away

and then the day came that all trying failed
words failed
the tongues
and the eyes
a supernova fell from the sky
and something fragile, curled under a leaf,
shivering and wild-eyed under sudden winter,
caught a warmer current
kissed me on the cheek
and flew away

seasons will change

seasons will change
said the sea to the stone
an impossible gray choked the sky
our hearts were lead under promise of thunderstorms
squalls lasting for days, echoing for weeks longer.

it was here we learned of metal and the
symphonies of concrete
the secrets of streets and lampposts and
loud noises and human kindness.
here we filled ourselves with smoke and copper
to burn the wick a brighter shade.

one day that familiar door will open again
and the ethereal midnight bats,
the rainbow shards of wax,
of dreams,
of youth and of being there,
will be born again in you,
in colors you can't even imagine.

II. spring
baby's breath, broken concrete

ripe

until you come and find me
I will sink into the earth
the jackals
the calm

you know me by sweat now
a haze behind your moon eyes
we ripen here in strawberry
cut our grateful lips on nectar

the earth
the jackals
the calm

come and find me
I will ache inside your magic
bleed it out in flood and sky

lily

I am an exploding sun
I am the milk inside your stars
the stutter in your dragon breath
a lily thirsty at midnight

moon and cicada
nature's copper dream

Persephone

Lily girl, you skip up the sky and land face-first in cloud milk. It's warm up here, it blankets, and it only chokes a little at first. Then you surrender to slow breath and clover, the blue clover of impossible springtime

You meet him by the river
That golden poet with those eyes
You offer him your lilies
He offers you a sonnet and you drink
You plan to meet again tomorrow but
The water is rising

You awaken in a peach pit with a whispering man
He calls himself death and you believe him
He worms your sonnet heart as he enters
You learn to speak insect, you carry the worms,
Feed them, let them breed

Your mother tried to find you but she's dead now
Far too many years between the lily and the seed
You call the names of all the highways
They listen but they do not breathe

Persephone, I'm sorry
I couldn't keep your boy at home
I couldn't tell him of your sorrow
He would have wept himself to bone

And now we wait here for the devil
To give us matchsticks for our chores
What do we do with them?

We'll tell you
We spell out sonnets on the floor.

leaf

bristled lights evaporate into hermit shells, white homes
ridged and shining.
there was a bell here once and the cold breath of concrete
. . . before the patient ivy took over and swam.

drip-notes, staccato, integrated fingers. at last a star
beckons from its nest,

come closer, wing tip, and find me.

one more nestles among the branches.
purple.
leaflike.
whistles when you're close.

faescapes

here's where the shimmer
goes to coagulate
smooth the black holes
find their eyes

underneath the fire
far from any unknown home
she is smoke held down
by flesh and fiber

iced, winged, fossilized
beneath impatient rivers
centuries of teeth
to chew the skies

oceans

I)

pearl drop visions out of empty eyes
luminous, scooped
a thin jelly film remains
sparkling,
remembering the eye.

swept away in mad pink fire
searing, fluorescent,
beautiful edges,
numb yellow morning.

II)

I dream red ocean here
silk-soft hues with jagged semitone connectors
raise voices, wet lips,
move the darkened water.

III)

my hand is buried in the sand
I open it and find your face inside
you've been there all along.

from mollusk days to crystal rainwater meditations in weird skins,
lion—carrot—sky,
blended watercolor pancake.

whose face?

yours?
mine?

IV.

the underwater city
more and more are washing up on shore
crimsoned, pickled sons, daughters,
all sway in choral surrender.

water waits for winter and the surface sleeps
below the fish shimmer
soak in sun flashes
bodies quick, slickened.

V.

you made the rain
we all came
drank and danced in pools of our bleeding
until we became
liquid salt.

etchings on the golem of fallen stars

their eyes were fire in the morning
they stood
swept up the ashes
and moved along.

I.

some purple planet hospitable to tropical life

the longest, loveliest day

majestic skeletons looming over the
mirage of tiny lifeforms . . .

light pouring in through the holes.

II.

the only one on a Sunday
new moon on Saturday afternoon

the sand felt so soft underneath our feet

we sank in sweaty liquors and
you told me of gray butterflies

the colors never stopped.

III.

we could breathe water together
exhale through our ears

inhale by tongue and fireflesh
carve mountains from night

IV.

the dance swallows everything
the bees bounce along like deaf corpses

the quickening tar of dreams
one jump in every direction

the opening of a door . . .

V.

those tiny, glowing things you still sing hymns to in the
night

the black tangent lightways
now you turned the lights off still . . .

staring gape-eyed, stormy
love affair with deafening black

moisture collecting on the cement floor.

VI.

landlocked Odysseus of darkness
lost the will to come home
the witch was the climax of his story
she frightened him and ate his heart
left hers in its place, festering

I wish for May and cough up autumn.

VII.

my wings are growing
little cartilage veins fill with life

. . . the bone densities of dreams.

VIII.

reshape me from molten rainbow

you cut and I destroy

the Great Volcano

the black sun

firefly.

IX.

the infinite in everything
so many sets of eyes . . .

X.

the rocks flush with sunrise
clouds part and the rains begin.

quiet

keep me here in feral moonlight
the birch trees shiver where it's dark
find me through leaves of apple
honey spire down a tongue dream

alien shards of volcanic crystal
windswept quiet a droplet of sea
only rhythm
siren and blood tide

midnight

a song now for a warm dream
let it be nectar, ripe and long
an entire open sun
the liquid mouths of stars
flickers under doorways

openings in catacombs
feathers litter this endless highway

open here in slow burn
take off this weathered time
your memories of animals
the legends in your eyes

midnight under fractured branches
canopies of broken artery,
nightmare vein
someday this will crystallize
a desert mouth will fill with rain

we can be stars now

I know you like I know the moon
by constellations you trace
over my eyes in glowing water

I want you like blood and music—
all the crimson lights you open
in our lithe horizons

together we arrange the bones,
lounge gold along each climax

all the stars we soak in wine,
lick clean by morning
dissolve with me
in grateful, aching rain

especially when the lights go out
we know by taste
just how to find this

please fill me with your sweat-
soaked darkness,
send each recurring nightmare
as thunder back to sky

**III. summer
violets in blind sun**

that summer

She grows much older that summer. All amber and chlorophyll, she peels from her roots, lets her branches furl across forest in veins and rivers. Finds tesseract and pearl tooth hiding among willows, amphibious stars crackle for the choke point.

In summer she evaporates, multiplies in prism, a gallery of refractions. She gazes into train lights and refuses. I'm tired, she tells them, spills out a dusty road instead, swaps her feet for years of windstorms. They say she lives here still, always howling. Until the day no one remembers, she echoes nightingale beneath your trees.

Dim memory lights and fissures in our boneyards. All oceans filled with swollen death, the mermaids left for orchid water long ago.

Before the sun there was a poem here, verses sunk in soapstone, etched in gold. Each syllable a cut in time. Now the timeworn lines have found a doorway, loosened their ankle ties, but incantations fade and calcify with parallels, an undead choral prophecy.

It always ends this way—the heavy dragon eats its tail in mired calculations. Always the sun rolling down the same mountain, that same weightless mountain where time and love move together but refuse to make eye contact, sleep rigid on opposite sides of the bed, the sheets soaked in pleading. The same nightmare cycles again.

Each razor story, every gray, splintered home. Each tall rooftop bent by this deafening momentum, this entropy dance of meat clinging to skeleton, these endless days of wheat and water.

All of this, alive in tapestry. Hungry for bones and hearts and holes through inertia. She grows much older that summer. Eats from fruit trees and falls asleep a stream. An ocean someday, a sun cascading down mountains. The moon rises here in whispers still; bright stars spin awake behind the haze.

voices

for Maria

a silhouette of ghosts
etching out the days
in sweat and meadow

*

someday, somewhere,
our poems will form a sea
and our voices can live

*

as a bird, or a canyon,
or two dozen black roses
a voice in all directions
loud and present.

lean back

lean back, pretty, and let your hair defy gravity
lean back, star child, and open your legs to the cosmic tongues

(if it hurts, bite down on chamomile)

never separate the berry from the vine
learn from the animals
the big-eyed deer and the locust
walk slowly, tiptoe
until the blood turns green again.

warm your face under crackling LEDs
no battery can hold you now

lean back, and let stone be your scepter
dive in, and find the shore.

split your lips under wrecking ball sun
lean back, dollface, it's never over.

angel hell

fluorescent lights pierce the crescent dream,
each haze washes down in
resonance and symmetry
swim these moons up my dying throat,
all lung rivers gasp,
clean past the zenith

speak to me in languages you buried
with your childhood, tell the dogs to run and
come back full of summer
tell the sun to freeze again til morning
I tell myself it's safe here
in a hungry mouth

deep water closes over the choke point
cradles us in ancient,
song and sea
shadows on the walls, broken monuments
lost time weeps, curls up in corners

capillaries strum alive, hum crescendo
tuned to hollow bone, they moan all night while
I bargain with memory,
claw at roadkill totems splayed on asphalt
no one else ever notices
no one comes outside to move the bodies

wash the blood and paint, an entrance here:
a dimension of teeth and stars
this angel hell, see how we writhe in sickle-wing,
scraped-jaw harmonies?
an ash planet waits for chrysalis

only mouths where we're going, angel hell
blisters and cut limbs, all our
knifework sings this place
your dead demons inside breathing still,
this belly of infinity, open sore aches
through lifetimes,
back to embryo,
back to fresh muscle til vibrato,
all flesh and cracked desert,
no water in sight.

easier

it's easier when no one loves me
I scream at the walls here alone
plaster peels slowly around me
in my sad rubber house

the open road

everyone wants the open road
that lonely, freezing highway
everyone wants the blood drums
the thunder flooding back

everyone wants the mortar here
to crush the wings of insects
everyone wants the end
tarred fairy-tale apocalypses
reverberating blood drums
it's dark in here
the drums are clean

all drums clean rhythm to a saw bone
a strange insect outside, those wings turn powder under
fragile snow
each flake stands on end like hair like spine like tidal wave
this time glistening rabbits, hungry boys, wide-eyed girls
asunder in torn dresses, all the lights and spines and
rabbits swallow thunder on the bone road, the bone
dream. the drums still clean

it rained the other day, here under the thunder, freezing
bone road to highway, slick-jawed destiny. up some tar
mountains and past the infinity horizon she shakes teeth
with sad devils on an overpass. they sit and drink awhile,
always a bottle or two of that thickness. soon say their
goodbyes, trace lit constellations back to city

back to city, back to skeleton
it's dark in here
the tails of star apocalypses

everyone wants the open road
those crackling, peeled-back highways
everyone wants the salt

laps

and so I lapped up the crumbs of all of it, every dead-ditch road forking off the main equator. a single line stretching a continent, blurred over waterways, mountainous over our homes.

there is no exit here a whirring repetition, some rehashed philosophy dressed in neon rags. some hearts fall through the gutters, collect at the bottom for late rodent excavation.

who wanted this? who looked down from a high chair and threw all our hope to the floor? there is still no exit here and I lapped the equator crumbs of dead forks in a ditch home, that place where rodents sleep awhile, forgetting.

blurred over the waterways
stretching a continent
stretched over still
a whirring repetition

hell

hell is just a desert
making love to fire

breathe

say you're sorry
say it until your eyes turn black
when they're black,
throw them in the fire.

say you're frightened
tell the mountain to pierce the sky
how do we find its heart, anyway?

say you're angry
say you're a wounded dog with no water
say you found the water and forgot you were the dog
unacceptable.
start from the beginning.

say you're not ready
tell the clock to wait a few days
lie on the kitchen floor
crack an egg or two
move onto the carpet.

say you never grew up
say you want nothing
but an open door and an ice cream cone
a skipping rope, a stone.

say you are the fire
everything that burns just got in the way
make peace with water
stop at the shore and smoke.

say you climbed way up a tree

but couldn't quite climb down
would your hands become the branches?
would your legs feel right at home?

the birds would laugh at you
cover you in feathers, tell you to fly
say you flew—
wouldn't that surprise them?

say you couldn't breathe
would the water welcome you?
would the weeds braid a pillow from your hair?
would you lie down at the bottom?
would you sleep?

say you're sorry
keep breathing
don't breathe

IV. fall
hibiscus, orange-red

your blood

I want to live inside your blood
the layer that coagulates and
dries at daybreak
blends into soil under
root and animal dream

all the insects will know me then
the rot inside my open mouth
will seep into their newborn creatures

you'll know me by the time we awaken
the forest is my vertigo,
spiral tongues alive and waiting
time trickles into slumber
into meals and cyclical
amusements
into cloud cover and rhythm

the white noise of a quiet life
muffled amputations near the fires
there is no other place to rest
no quick evolution for
an aching skeleton

only this
and us
and miles
all time and noise and bleeding seasons
the insects pollinate their homes
feed on this sweetness of
ripe petals
clinging to an empty core, they

shiver under autumn's
leaden sun

spool

Go on, trace the cracks on your suit of armor, like a wolf moon, like an apostrophe. They belong to us and we eat them alive so they can grow, so they can ribbon into dust, a rainbow, a plethora of soil. Trace the light inside through chipped teeth, slide like butter down the freeway. The birds left early this year and were replaced by dynamite. The squirrels are fat and confused and don't know whether to sleep or swim. Don't even get me started on the fish.

Leap year and the windows freeze over. We all buckle into the couch. Throw planets around the living room, stand on our heads in jello molds, waiting to evolve. Then that grows tiresome and we begin shouting in new languages at each other, each exploding ten thousand times per second, per syllable. The children are all monsters but we forgive them, somehow, but never forget. We're just waiting for them to dissolve into something human, something real between the bones will possess them and boy will that be a relief.

All the newspapers catch fire and the smoke gives way to chants, marches, hashtags . . . all those little things we like to use to distract ourselves. It's always been this way, really . . . a stone isn't always a stone isn't always a memory doesn't always carry moss. For years now it's been easier to dive into molasses but what do we have to show for it? Just ask the fish . . .

Forever rains over our eyes and we absorb, lithe and motionless here in the infinity. Hard to reconcile with colors and shapes these days, for every one that lights up another slides down the drain, and we forget. The birds have long memories they say, they keep coming back, content to leave feathers behind and huddle in the frost until the cold reaches critical mass. "Content" may not be the right word but bird isn't one of my languages and they wouldn't tell me their secrets anyway.

The trees collide with the sun, then the colors come back again.

Rivers will lead you right back where you forgot you were lost.

The burnt orange trees hand me a basket of variables. I shake it up and some fall on the ground, sprout into weird hydras that sing in vibrato. Everything here looks perfect and wet and the ocean's really not too far, you can see it when you close your eyes. As for me, I ride a ghost ship back and forth on dream lilies, sometimes substituting lilacs as needed.

Lavender is the color of the spaceship that took away the lightswitch. The beings on board wanted to milk electricity to reverse engineer astral agriculture. We'll never know if the experiment worked, they're not coming back here anytime soon, too many mosquitoes.

Then the rains come down like breathing (yes the same ones) and the oranges all fall off the trees and the honeysuckle comes a bit too close for comfort and we awaken with nebulas stroking our cheeks.

Bring back the pearls, the oysters are too weak to fight back. Cracked shells usher in a new underwater century. They're plotting right now.

What is time when the clocks don't work?

I think there's something green and omniscient in the microwave. It eats radiation and writes novellas in its spare time.

We're all just planets here, multiplying planets. The erosion is the best part.

I am the starry eyed penultimate garden gnome you forgot to take inside.

I am the subcutaneous river otter that won't let you sleep.

I am a spool of capillary.

hello

I make you uncomfortable.
I approach you with
wing-eyes
and a large,
fibrous voice.
part man, part spider, part light.

you die alone

*how does it feel
the moment
you die alone?*

she watches her chest
rise and fall, her salt breath
torn in sputters.

the mermaid kisses her lips,
all cold and blue and
buoyant.

*how does it feel
the moment
you let your heart
die alone
at the bottom?*

she looks through her, blue
eyes stained with storm.

*like I had drowned,
and the drowning
was done,
and the rain
was over.
now my heart can
die alone
again tomorrow.
and the next day.
and all the endless days we
die alone.*

she rises from the shore,
limps her way toward the city,
both ragged lungs alive.

the mermaid coughs,
an ice wind through
scale and bone,
dreams of hearth
and fire.

the star side (it flew back)

I thought you had left me, little dungeon bird
but the blue still shines across the river.

thought it was ten feet down a snare, but it was eight
a small yet significant miscalculation
I thought you had left me I thought I was shattered
doomed to never stroke the words again like honeyed
beams of everfucking love, everfucking play, play til I drop
and you dissolve around me a star explosion, nebula of
love, sight love everything and the world is new, the world
dissolved and the world littered and spilled around us and
poured out a grave. a new grave. ours.

(and we sat there and wept because it was white and the
honey died ashes from our throats)

it was ours and we swallowed it.
it was all we knew.
it was all we loved and we kept it
between our knees in our warm beds.

warm love, a twisted river
always looks warm from the star side.

I thought you had left me, little dungeon bird
but the blue still shines across the river.

pinhead

sometimes my chest is a thousand butterflies
and I keep spinning off to where I'm off to

the shifting oasis
sandstorms for miles

there in the center-eye, the thing we belong to
ashes for days again, maybe weeks this time

someday the long game, the novel, the whole world
will be written

it all rests upon a pin

flower moon

nothing to everything coated in petals
iridescent ash violet, mute blood eye expands,
floats behind shadow.

*(I have too much energy, but I know how to swim
to float eons on my back in night waters
and I'll show you if you bring your violets.)*

marsh unfolding and the heroes died
but they were smiling
safe, inside their halos.

fire came fast and their sons all fought
destroyed the threat and quenched the chaos
and the animals and man lived together at last
or wasn't that the story?

maybe sometimes the hero lives
sometimes the hero lives a long time
whether deep in hollow caves
at the call of the witch, or sirens,
or at war with invisible tapestries
or with himself?

or, sometimes, just sometimes,
the hero will rise, and live, and slay all the monsters
the village is safe and the children are happy
and everyone can be heard laughing
the mountains feel taller and grow close to the stars.

mountains may fall and the cities fall sooner
but there is a thing that survives

something that lives in flower moons above the water
the wind gusts and a new life folds over.

one of these days the shadow will clear
we will be ready.

flightless

all of this belongs to autumn
heavy rain doesn't cease
when she's constricted
nor do the flowers look away
as they're cut, arranged
lithe and dying,
crushed in extravagant
mortars under
cyclical, laughing,
burgundy skies

these gray beaches stretch
on for years
sleepless waves roar
just behind the searching eye
do we ever get to
crystallize?
does anyone ever really
get home?
is it all a time-bent wasteland
where we live as caricatures?
is the ecstatic capillary
somehow enough? our
bleeding of primary colors
into the ground?
coastlines recede through
my avian dreams . . .

flightless and mouthless
a bed of white salt
all the colors,
the absence of color

all the colors,
the absence of stars

worlds

in the center of the great sun
no one is cold or hungry
colors intertwine in ribbons
tentacle between us all

ashes never fall on open hands
the green things never wither
water flows for eons
and we sing leopards
onto the spotted Earth

the continents are glowing;
a prism of voice and heart

look for us in open water
we collide as light-soaked mirrors
each shard a promise of tapestry

dream, a forum for symphony
our blood the copper ocean
we swim through the hours
scooping out the pores

we are a world of salt
we are a world of candles

always

I've lived too many years
here as a dead thing
just to die now
an alias in oil slick,
dangling gray
and trudging fog
the summer winds we shape
at dawn, the mysteries
ours to wander
the animal and nebula
wings open,
warm and bright . . .

you found me sunk in
nightmare, haunted
lips and leaden sorrow
yearning for the fires
under amber-colored sky
meadow-heavy oxygen
had drowned me until hollow
drained me into nectar,
a lilied, faded star

I called each corpse to dirt
and still they flailed here,
waving torches
sizzling in circumstance,
the pyres they'd blown wide
all marionette distractions
and the guilty, jaded liars
the architectured pity
disillusioned,

downcast eyes

seasons scatter dust away
and everything that's leaving
our paradise keeps bleeding,
electric through the holes
illuminating what we need
it finds us
stunned and blinded,
whether making
love to night or sorting
ashes on the floors

it's all a theatre, isn't it? the
curtain wide and grinning
Shakespeare's merry fool recites
that timeless speech again
we laugh and we corrode
and then we
fold it into pages
close our eyes, pretending that
it's all a winged dream . . .

what is our winged dream but
everything we see before us?
everything we know but
fear admit to time or soul?
we open up the embers
cast in centuries
of frostbite
disintegrate the stars
as we begin becoming whole . . .

we are here each other's

and there is no way to leave it
no way not to see it
no way not to
flood the vein
we already know
and so every ocean knows it
all that always was and
all the ways we'll fly again

everything we are, and
all the ways we'll fly again

PUBLISHER'S NOTE

For queries on any of our titles or scheduled publications, and to submit creative work, contact us at roguewolfpress@gmail.com.

We are interested in art (poetry, prose, visual, and experimental amalgamations)—forged in vein and bone marrow. Send us your underworld vagabond tales, your crystalline viscera, and all the times you scraped yourself on elated, jealous stars. We like our art and poetry alive.

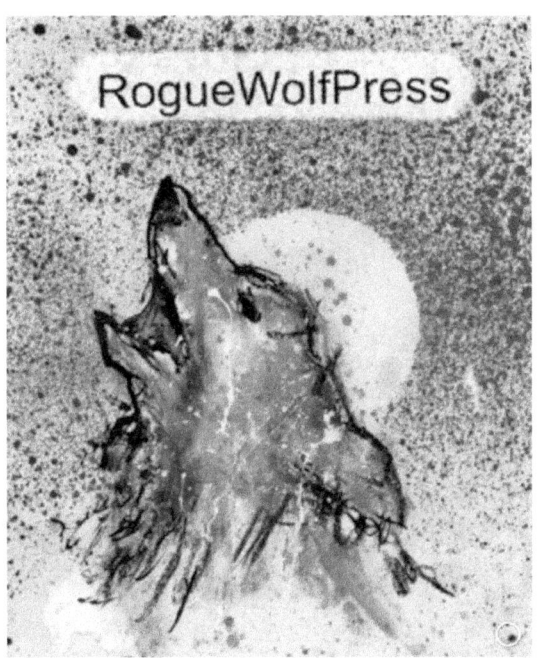

Forget form and ritual, forget the academic platitudes—it's the Second Renaissance, and we create our own traditions here. Time for the real, and the new.

—*Rogue Wolf and Ghost, Editors, Rogue Wolf Press*

www.ingramcontent.com/pod-product-compliance
Lightning Source LLC
Chambersburg PA
CBHW070848220526
45466CB00005B/1925